Essentials of Managed Health Care Study Guide

Fifth Edition

Peter R. Kongstvedt, MD

JONES AND BARTLETT PUBLISHERS
Sudbury, Massachusetts
BOSTON TORONTO LONDON SINGAPORE

World Headquarters
Jones and Bartlett Publishers
40 Tall Pine Drive
Sudbury, MA 01776
978-443-5000
info@jbpub.com
www.jbpub.com

Jones and Bartlett Publishers
Canada
6339 Ormindale Way
Mississauga, Ontario L5V 1J2
Canada

Jones and Bartlett Publishers
International
Barb House, Barb Mews
London W6 7PA
United Kingdom

Jones and Bartlett's books and products are available through most bookstores and online booksellers. To contact Jones and Bartlett Publishers directly, call 800-832-0034, fax 978-443-8000, or visit our website www.jbpub.com.

Substantial discounts on bulk quantities of Jones and Bartlett's publications are available to corporations, professional associations, and other qualified organizations. For details and specific discount information, contact the special sales department at Jones and Bartlett via the above contact information or send an email to specialsales@jbpub.com.

ISBN-13: 9780763764319

Production Credits
Publisher: Michael Brown
Production Director: Amy Rose
Associate Editor: Katey Birtcher
Editorial Assistant: Catie Heverling
Production Editor: Tracey Chapman
Production Assistant: Roya Millard
Marketing Manager: Sophie Fleck
Manufacturing and Inventory Control Supervisor: Amy Bacus
Composition: Auburn Associates, Inc.
Cover Design: Brian Moore
Cover Image Design: Kate Ternullo
Printing and Binding: Malloy, Inc.
Cover Printing: Malloy, Inc.

6048
Printed in the United States of America
12 11 10 09 08 10 9 8 7 6 5 4 3 2 1

Contents

Part 4: Operational Management and Marketing

Part 5: Special Markets

Part 6: Legal and Regulatory Issues

Notes

CHAPTER 1

The Origins of Managed Health Care

CHAPTER STUDY REVIEW

1. The first managed care system can be traced back to 1910 and the Western Clinic, which many cite as the first example of a health maintenance organization (HMO). One of the first health insurance plans was implemented at Baylor Hospital in Houston, Texas, in 1929. Despite the AMA's 1932 declaration against prepaid group practices, managed care plans continued to gain popularity. With the increasing commonality of managed care plans came greater legislative involvement. A major boost to the HMO movement was the 1973 federal HMO Act. Two other major pieces of legislation affecting the managed care field were the Health Insurance Portability and Accountability Act (HIPAA) of 1996 and the Balanced Budget Act of 1997. Today, multistate managed care firms dominate the market, reflecting a trend toward consolidation. Most Americans with health care coverage are covered by some form of managed care plan.
2. Three areas of innovation in managed care are:
   - Collaboration between physicians and hospitals to form physician-hospital organizations (PHOs)
   - The development of carve-outs
   - Advances made possible by computer technology
3. Managed care has matured considerably since its modest beginnings. Three aspects of the maturation of managed care are:
   - **HMO and PPO growth**. HMOs and PPOs grew exponentially as employers came to rely on managed care at the expense of once-traditional indemnity insurance plans. Medicare and Medicaid programs contracted increasingly with HMOs as well. However, HMO enrollment began to decline in the 1990s, and that trend has continued. In contrast, PPOs have grown.
   - **External oversight activities**. In 1991, the National Committee for Quality Assurance (NCQA) began to accredit HMOs. Today, many employers look favorably upon, sometimes even demand, NCQA accreditation.

Notes

- **Shift in focus of cost management efforts**. Inpatient hospital utilization is still scrutinized, but more notice is being taken of ambulatory services. Managed care has also moved away from tight "command and control" of all services in order to concentrate on more expensive aspects of care.

4. The following are the three main aspects of the restructuring that have taken place in managed care:
   - **Blurred distinctions among plans**. The managed care environment is becoming increasingly complicated as organizations become hybridized.
   - **Decreasing role of primary care physicians (PCPs)**. In managed care organizations, PCPs assumed responsibility for the allocation of resources and rose above specialists and hospitals in importance. However, with the decline of HMOs, as well as a reduction of the use of PCP "gatekeeper" models by many HMOs, the role of the PCP, while still very important, is no longer paramount. However, managed care of all forms encourages the use of primary care over specialty care.
   - **Consolidation among plans and providers**. Large, multistate care organizations account for the vast majority of national enrollment, and there is no end in sight to the current trend toward mergers.
5. More recent changes in managed care include the following:
   - **Backlash against managed care**. The public backlash against managed care has been fueled by the media and politicians. The public and providers were opposed to precertification and authorization requirements, as well as the use of restricted networks. Managed care plans contributed to this backlash through increasingly bureaucratic mechanisms for managing healthcare costs, as well as the conversion of many health plans to for-profit status. This backlash has subsided recently, in parallel with the decline of tighter forms of managed care.
   - **Return of health-cost inflation**. At the same time that managed care moved away from more restrictive models, healthcare cost inflation began to surge. This is not only due to the use of wider networks and less restrictive access to care, but also to evolving new medical interventions, such as technology, devices, drugs, diagnostic modalities, and treatment options.
   - **Appearance of new types of plans**. New types of health plans have begun to emerge, mostly those centered around consumer-directed health care. Greater cost sharing by consumers, combined with more access to cost and quality data, is intended to make consumers more active in managing their own health and healthcare resources. Greater cost sharing by consumers is appearing in most types of health plans as well.

Notes

CHAPTER 2

Types of Managed Care Organizations and Integrated Healthcare Delivery Systems

CHAPTER STUDY REVIEW

1. There are many types of managed care plans. Each was designed to fulfill a specific set of needs, and each has inherent strengths and weaknesses.
2. Indemnity insurance simply provides insurance against financial loss (i.e., it indemnifies against loss).
3. A service plan is similar to indemnity insurance, but with the added feature of a network of providers under contract with the plan. The contract provides for specific reimbursement schedules and the contracted provider agrees to abide by them.
4. Indemnity insurance and service plan companies developed managed care–type overlays to provide both cost control and freedom of choice. The four types of managed care overlays are general utilization management; specialty utilization management; catastrophic, or large-case, management; and workers' compensation utilization management. None of these are as effective as other types of managed care plans, however.
5. **Prefered provider organizations** (PPOs) typically create a provider network for covered individuals by contracting directly with hospitals, physicians, and diagnostic facilities. Unlike HMOs, PPOs allow members to use non–PPO providers, but apply higher coinsurance rates or deductibles for out-of-network services. Many PPOs have utilization management programs.
6. **Exclusive provider organizations** (EPOs) are similar in organization and purpose to PPOs. Members can use participating providers for all healthcare services, but the plan generally does not reimburse

Notes

patients for services received outside of the network. EPOs are now quite rare.

7. **Point-of-service** (POS) plans are hybrids of traditional HMO and PPO plans.
   - **Primary care PPOs**. Primary care physicians act as gatekeepers for referrals and institutional services. Patients have some coverage for services not authorized by the primary care physician or delivered out of network, but coverage is usually significantly lower than for in-network providers.
   - **POS HMOs**. These provide some level of indemnity-type coverage for members, who can choose which plan to use for each instance of care.
8. **Health Maintenance Organizations** (HMOs) are organized healthcare systems that are responsible for financing and delivering a range of comprehensive health services. Some HMOs use prepaid fixed fees, and all must ensure that members have access to covered services. The differences among HMO plans pertain to relationships between the plans and participating physicians.
   - **Staff model**. Physicians are employed by the HMO and are typically paid on a salary basis. These plans include physicians in common specialties to provide for members' various needs. Patients cannot use out-of-network physicians. Now uncommon.
   - **Group model**. The plan contracts with a multispecialty physician group practice. The physicians are employed by, or partners in the practice, not the HMO. These groups may be either captive or independent. This plan also provides a limited choice of participating physicians.
   - **Network model**. The plan contracts with more than one physician group. These may be broad-based multispecialty groups or small groups, representing different specialties. The group is responsible for providing all healthcare services for patients. Physicians can refer to other physicians, as necessary. These groups may be either closed or open panel. Mostly found in the Western U.S.
   - **IPA model**. The plan contracts with associations of physicians to provide services for members. This open-panel plan includes a broad range of physicians from various specialties. IPAs create organized forums for physicians to negotiate as a group with HMOs.
   - **Direct contract model**. Similar to the IPA model, the plan contracts directly with individual physicians. The plan recruits broad panels of community physicians, both primary care and specialists, to participate as plan providers.
   - **Open access HMOs**. This model does not require a primary care physician or gatekeeper. There may be a financial incentive for

Notes

patients to see primary care physicians for referrals, but this is not required.

9. Funding differences. MCO's are paid two different ways.
   - **Self-insured**. In this model, the MCO receives a fixed monthly payment to cover administrative services and the employer is responsible for the actual expenses made by the MCO for health services. A settlement process often occurs at the end of specified periods in which a final payment is calculated.
   - **Experience related**. The MCO receives monthly premium payments based on prior utilization and cost of its group to reach a final premium rate. Refunds are calculated and made to the appropriate party.
10. Consumer-directed health plans (CDHPs) have evolved in recent years. Such plans combine a high-deductible health insurance policy with some form of pretax fund, such as a health reimbursement account or a health savings account. Consumers are responsible for any costs not covered by insurance or these accounts. Consumers usually have access to a PPO network as well. Such plans strive to make information on cost and quality available to consumers to help them make decisions.
11. An integrated delivery system (IDS) is created when more than one type of provider comes together in a legal structure to manage health care. The goal of an IDS is to improve efficiency in managing healthcare delivery.
12. There are three basic structures of an IDS:
    - Systems in which only physicians are integrated
    - Systems in which physicians are integrated with facilities
    - Systems that include insurance functions

    All of the following increase in moving from the first to the third structure: the degree of integration and potential ability to operate in a managed care environment, the complexity of formation and operation, the required capital investment, and the surrounding political difficulties.
13. There are many IDS types; each has its advantages and disadvantages:
    - Independent practice association (**IPA**). An IPA is a legal entity composed of independent physicians who contract with the IPA primarily to have it contract with one or more MCOs. IPAs offer a broad choice of physicians and require less startup capital than some other IDSs. However, IPAs can be unwieldy, because they comprise a large body of physicians with little in common. They also are unable to leverage resources, achieve economies of scale, or significantly change behavior.
    - Physician practice management company (**PPMC**). PPMCs comprise physicians only, without the involvement of a hospital.

Notes

These groups can be either for-profit, comprehensive PPMCs, or specialty PPMCs. Regardless of the type, their sole purpose is to manage physicians' practices. However, PPMCs do not have a good track record, creating an atmosphere of distrust.

- Group practice without walls (**GPWW**). A GPWW does not require the participation of a hospital and is often formed as a means for physicians to organize without hospital support. GPWWs are owned and governed by member physicians and have the legal ability to negotiate and commit on behalf of all members. These groups lack a significant ability to manage practice behavior, and they must continually seek out new sources of capital, information systems, and management expertise.
- Physician-hospital organization (**PHO**). PHOs allow a hospital and its physicians to negotiate with third-party payers. This type of IDS can be open or closed. A drawback of the PHO model is that it often is structured loosely and fails to actually improve contracting ability.
- Management services organization (**MSO**). MSOs offer both a vehicle for negotiating with MCOs and additional services to support physicians' practices. These groups bind physicians closer to hospitals and can bring economies of scale and professional management to physicians' office services. However, physicians can challenge allegiances with relative ease and these groups have limited ability to enact change.
- **Foundations**. This model can be formed when a hospital creates a not-for-profit foundation, purchases physicians' practices, and then places them within the foundation. Foundations are governed by boards not dominated by either hospital administrators or physicians. The foundation model provides a high level of structural integration and can satisfy legal constraints that prohibit hospitals from purchasing services or employing physicians. Unfortunately, the foundation model has a built-in potential for conflicts between hospitals and physician groups, and foundations must continually prove that they provide a benefit for the community to retain their nonprofit status.
- Provider sponsored organization (**PSO**). PSOs are cooperative ventures of group providers who control financial arrangements and health service delivery. Their focus is on the Medicare community. The need for reserves in this model has been greatly underestimated, and PSOs often do not have managerial or systems capabilities to administer the plans. PSOs, once popular, are now much less common.

Notes

CHAPTER 3

Elements of the Management Control and Governance Structure

CHAPTER STUDY REVIEW

1. A managed care organization's board of directors is responsible for the governance functions of the MCO. These functions include the following:
   - Final approval of corporate bylaws
   - General oversight of profitability or reserve status
   - Oversight and approval of significant fiscal events
   - Responsibility to protect shareholders' interest (in for-profit plans)
   - Review of reports and document signing
   - Setting and approving policy
   - Oversight of the quality management program
   - Hiring the CEO and reviewing his or her performance (in free-standing plans)
2. The board might face liability under certain circumstances. To avoid liability, board members must:
   - Exercise their duties to the benefit of the plan, not their own self-interest
   - Avoid personal conflict of interest
   - Operate within the plan bylaws
   - Exercise diligence in carrying out their duties
   - Understand all reports for which the board is responsible for attesting to
   - Have adequate liability insurance for acts of commission or omission; such insurance is routinely provided for by the plan
3. Managed care organizations have at least seven key management positions. These seven positions are as follows:
   - Executive director/chief operating officer
   - Medical director

Notes

- Finance director
- Marketing director
- Operations director
- Director of information systems
- Corporate compliance officer

4. Seven committees are crucial to the successful operation of MCOs:
- QM committee
- Credentialing committee
- Medical advisory committee
- Utilization review committee
- Pharmacy and therapeutics committee
- Medical grievance review committee
- Corporate compliance committee

Notes

Chapter 4

Examining Common Assertions about Managed Care

CHAPTER STUDY REVIEW

1. A number of theories have been offered regarding the widespread adoption of managed care. Some believe that it has been a response to rising healthcare costs. Others believe that it is a result of problems with the quality of health care, including underuse, overuse, misuse, and geographic variation.
2. Much of the political debate surrounding managed care has revolved around claims concerning the treatment of particular individuals' cases. Conversely, when consumers are asked directly about the quality of their personal health care, most express satisfaction.
3. Many common myths surround the issue of managed care. For each myth, there is either evidence that proves it false or little evidence is available to substantiate it.
   - **Myth**: Most people do not like their health insurance plan.
   - **Myth**: The growth of managed care health systems has restricted choice.
   - **Myth**: Members enrolled in managed care plans receive lower-quality services than those with traditional indemnity coverage.
   - **Myth**: Doctors' decisions on necessary treatment often are overruled by utilization-review personnel.
   - **Myth**: Health insurance plans' profit margins are largely responsible for the rising cost of health insurance.
   - **Myth**: Health insurance plans' administrative costs consume a large portion of the premium dollar.
   - **Myth**: Managed care has not lived up to its promise to control skyrocketing healthcare costs.
   - **Myth**: Managed care plans avoid enrolling sick patients and achieve high quality and positive outcomes by enrolling healthier members.

Notes

- **Myth**: Managed care fails to add any value to the healthcare system and plays a small role in improving the health of Americans.

4. Evidence shows that managed care has helped lower healthcare costs and has made health care more widely available.
5. Before the advent of managed care, few in the healthcare industry were subject to measures of quality. With the growth in managed care enrollment, many aspects of the healthcare delivery system are now subject to rigorous quality assessment measures.

Notes

CHAPTER 5

Physician Networks in Managed Health Care

CHAPTER STUDY REVIEW

1. Depending on their qualifications, physicians can be designated as primary or specialty care physicians (PCP or SCP), or sometimes both. In many HMOs, the PCP acts as a gatekeeper, authorizing referrals to specialists when necessary.
2. Most healthcare systems consider the following three specialties as primary care providers: family practice, internal medicine, and pediatrics. In some rural or underserved areas, general practitioners also are considered primary care physicians. All types of managed care plans allow direct access to OB/Gyn for women.
3. Hospital-based physicians include:
   - Radiology
   - Anesthesiology
   - Pathology
   - Hospitalist
4. Nonphysician clinicians (NPCs) or mid-level practitioners (MLPs) capable of providing primary care include Physician Assistants (PAs) and Nurse Practitioners (NPs).
5. Some plans place specialty networks into different tiers. Different levels of coverage apply based on what tier the physician is in.
6. In creating a provider network, MCOs must take into consideration a variety of factors, including access needs and geographic requirements, needs of plan members, and the variety of practitioners.
7. When developing a network, open-panel MCOs often have to deal with a variety of contracting situations. Each situation has relative advantages and disadvantages. The various contracting situations include the following:
   - **Individual physicians**. This is the most common category in open-panel MCOs. Individual physicians contract directly with the health plan.

Notes

- **Medical groups**. Small groups operate as cohesive units in order to contract with MCOs.
- **IPAs**. Legal entities that contract with physicians and then act as the negotiating body between the physicians and the MCO.
- **Specialty management companies**. These are companies that manage specific specialties. They are paid by the health plan, and they, in turn, pay the specialists. Such companies often accept risk.
- **IDS**. An independent delivery system that can be hospital based or limited to physicians.
- **FPP**. Faculty practice plans are organized around teaching programs and are usually found at university hospitals.
- **Retail health clinics**. Clinics in convenient locations, such as a drug store. They provide simple primary care using mid-level practitioners.

8. MCOs credential physicians to ensure a level of quality and acceptability among their physicians and to protect themselves from potential liability should a dispute arise regarding a certain provider. Credentialing is first carried out during the recruiting process and includes significant background checks regarding issues such as prior claims, training, and status according to national data banks. Recredentialing occurs every two years in most cases. Credentialing can be performed by a designated company that meets certain standards.

9. The National Provider Identifier (NPI) was created as part of HIPAA. All providers are required to use it as of 2008, and it replaces all other identifiers except providers' DEA (drug) and tax ID numbers. HIPAA also requires that any electronic commerce between physicians and a health plan must comply with certain standards regarding code sets and transaction format.

10. Physicians and their office staff must be oriented by the plan regarding policies and procedures.

11. Networks must be actively maintained to remain effective. Active maintenance often includes office evaluations, medical record review, electronic connectivity review, interaction with a provider's representative, and monitoring member services complaints.

12. In any plan, there will be physicians who will not or cannot work within the system and whose style of practice is cost-ineffective or of poor quality. Offending physicians might face sanctions or, in some cases, removal from the plan.

Notes

CHAPTER 6

Basic Compensation of Physicians in Managed Health Care

CHAPTER STUDY REVIEW

1. Managed care organizations use several methods to reimburse providers. Most MCOs use a mix of reimbursement methods rather than just one.
2. Capitation is a system of prepayment for services on a per-member, per-month basis (PMPM). Capitation rates can vary depending on such factors as age, gender, current health status, geography, and practice type. Capitation does not vary, however, based on the use of services by members. PCPs are more often capitated than SCPs, but both occur in HMOs. Only HMOs capitate.
3. A withhold system used by some HMOs entails the withholding of a percentage of the primary care physician's reimbursement each month (for capitation) or each payment (for FFS). In a capitation system, the primary care physician then receives a check each month in the amount of the capitation rate minus the withhold amount. If, at the end of the year, money has not been used to cover cost overruns, it is returned to the primary care physician.
4. When using capitation risk pools, services can be paid for through a variety of methods, but for accounting purposes the expense is drawn against a capitated fund or pool. The four broad categories of nonprimary care risk pools are referral, hospital, ancillary services, and "other." The flow of funds and level of risk for each pool may be handled differently.
5. For purposes of year-end reconciliation, it is common for a plan to stop deducting expenses from an individual primary care physician's pool after reaching a certain threshold. This is called stop-loss protection. The two forms of stop-loss protection are costs for individual members and aggregate cost protection. The expenses incurred after

Notes

the threshold is exceeded will be paid from an aggregate pool or a specially allocated stop-loss fund.

6. When plans track risk pools on an individual-risk basis, physicians are at risk for their own patients' medical costs. When risk pools are tracked on a pooled-risk basis, risk is distributed across the entire network.
7. Specialists are capitated in a variety of forms, including geographic capitation, contact capitation (though this has become uncommon), and other mechanisms that differ from how PCPs are capitated. Disease management or single-specialty management firms may also be capitated.
8. Under full-professional-risk capitation, a primary care physician or medical group receives money for all professional services, but not for hospital services. This method is generally supportable only by a large group or organized system of primary care physicians. Global capitation refers to the medical group or organized healthcare delivery system receiving capitation payment for all services, including institutional and other services, such as pharmacy. Global capitation can only be supported by large and sophisticated medical groups, and even then the track record of global capitation is poor in terms of financial outcomes.
9. Capitation payments must be adjusted for such things as changes in benefits design or for differing copayments and/or coinsurance.
10. HMOs choose capitation for a number of reasons. Capitation puts providers at some risk or incentive for medical expenses and utilization, eliminates the FFS incentive to overuse, brings financial incentives of providers in line with those of the HMO, and makes it easier to predict costs. Providers benefit from capitation through the assurance of cash flow, and in some cases profit margins exceed those of FFS.
11. Capitation does have drawbacks. A degree of chance is involved, especially when dealing with small numbers of members. Practices may forget that many members of a plan are not necessarily patients, so capitation payments can seem small compared to services rendered. Finally, the financial reward is temporally remote (i.e., remote in time) from the actual medical service, because the physician does not receive immediate payment.
12. In FFS plans, payment is distributed on the basis of expenditure of resources. Although many physicians prefer them, FFS plans are sometimes criticized because of the belief that physicians will do more if they are paid more. FFS can be either straight or performance-based.
13. In some plans, the negotiated contract provider payment rate is a percentage discount off the UCR or the submitted claim, whichever is lower. This is relatively rare now.

Notes

14. In a relative value scale (RVS) system, each procedure has associated with it a relative value. RVSs are very popular in FFS plans, but there has been a problem with the imbalance between the values of procedural and cognitive services. The Resource Based Relative Value Scale (RBRVS), developed by CMS, has been widely adopted to address this imbalance.
15. Global fees are single fees for all services that are delivered in an episode of care. These fees are variations on the FFS model and can be tied to performance.
16. Other forms of FFS include differences based on where the service was performed, mandatory reductions in fees, the use of withholds, and budgeted FFS.
17. Price transparency is a relatively recent phenomenon. Health plans are now posting the fees that they will pay providers for common types of services and providers, as well as estimated costs if a member goes out of network. This is intended to enable consumers to make informed choices.
18. The three main problems with the FFS model in managed care are churning, upcoding, and unbundling. Churning is when physicians perform more procedures than necessary and schedule patient visits at frequent intervals. Upcoding is a slow creep upward of CPT codes that pay more. Unbundling involves charging for services previously included in a single fee without lowering, or lowering sufficiently, the original fee.
19. Federal regulations that affect reimbursement are applicable only in federally funded health plans, with Medicare and Medicaid being the primary types of plans included. These regulations include the determination of whether a physician is at significant financial risk, the requirement of some form of stop-loss protection for the protection of physicians and physician groups, disclosure requirements for network providers who are at financial risk, and the conduct of customer satisfaction surveys by MCOs.

Notes

CHAPTER 7

Hospitals, Facilities, and Ancillary Services

CHAPTER STUDY REVIEW

1. Hospital contracting has become increasingly difficult for a variety of reasons. Hospitals have consolidated, giving them greater negotiating power. Hospital costs have sharply escalated due to advances in technology, a shortage of nurses and other clinical personnel, and a decline in the number of available hospital beds.
2. Developing a hospital network is a complex process involving six basic steps:
   - Selecting hospitals
   - Establishing general negotiating strategy
   - Developing data
   - Setting goals
   - Determining the responsibilities and roles of plan management
   - Determining the responsibilities and roles of hospital management
3. The plan may place different hospital networks into different tiers, providing higher benefits coverage for those members who use higher-tier hospitals.
4. Many reimbursement methods are possible when contracting with hospitals. In deciding which method to use, management must consider whether or not the plan's information systems are able to actually administer whatever financial terms the contract calls for.
   - Some plans reimburse via straight charges or a straight discount on charges. With a straight discount, the hospital submits its claim and the plan discounts it by an agreed-upon percentage.
   - A sliding-scale discount is a percentage discount that reflects the total volume of admissions and outpatient procedures.
   - A negotiated per diem is a single payment for a day in the hospital regardless of the actual charges or costs incurred. A sliding-scale per diem is based on total volume.
   - Per diem reimbursement can be combined with differential by day in hospital, whereby the first day is paid at a higher rate.

Notes

- Reimbursement may also differ if the patient is in an observation unit or a step-down unit.
- Most plans refuse to pay for expenses associated with so-called "never events"—serious medical errors that should never occur, such as amputating the wrong limb or a serious medication error.
- Diagnosis Related Groups (DRG) are a common reimbursement system whereby the plan negotiates a payment mechanism based on diagnosis, not charges. Often linked to Medicare or state-regulated rates.
- Service-related case rates are similar to DRGs, but in this case the hospital receives a flat per-admission reimbursement for the service for which the patient is admitted.
- Case rates and package pricing are set rates for certain categories of procedures.
- Capitation is the reimbursement of the hospital on a PMPM basis. Percentage of revenue, unlike capitation, can vary with the premium rate charged and the actual revenue yield.
- Contact capitation involves reimbursement in which the capitation is tied to the percentage of admissions to a hospital, with some adjustments for type of service provided. It is rare.
- Periodic Interim Payments (PIPs) and cash advances also are rare. Cash advances are replenished if they drop below a certain amount, providing hospitals with positive cash flow.
- Capitation is one form of performance-based reimbursement. Other forms include penalties, withholds, and service and quality incentives.

5. Separate types of contracts and reimbursement are applied for single-specialty hospitals. Health plans must also pay attention to the emergency department.
6. Reimbursement for outpatient procedures does not necessarily mirror that for inpatient services, but the two do have some methods in common.
   - Providers might be reimbursed through straight or sliding-scale discounts on charges.
   - Plans might negotiate package pricing or bundled charges for outpatient procedures.
   - Ambulatory visits might be reimbursed through APGs and APCs, which are similar to DRGs for inpatient services.
7. Pricing transparency refers to health plans posting information about hospital costs so that consumers can use that information to make informed choices.
8. Ancillary services are those that are provided as an adjunct to basic primary or specialty services. They include almost everything other than institutional services. Pharmacy services are a unique type of ancillary service.

Notes

9. Many ancillary services are carved out of the main medical delivery system, and the risk is transferred to another organization. These organizations can achieve economies of scale and manage overall cost and quality. Most plans place strict limits on ancillary services that are owned by physicians and who also order their use.
10. HMO plans that have absolute limitations on benefits provided for ancillary services often use capitation. Some plans, such as a POS, might use capitation only for in-network charges and pay out-of-network charges with regular fee allowances.

Notes

CHAPTER 8

Performance-Based Compensation in Managed Health Care

CHAPTER STUDY REVIEW

1. The fundamental goal of P4P is to align financial rewards with improvements in the use of evidence-based medical practice and safety in order to promote better outcomes as efficiently as possible.
2. The quality paradigm is:
   - Structure
   - Process
   - Outcome
3. The basic approach includes:
   - Choosing the measures
   - Accessing sources of data
   - Accessing applicable standards
4. Rewards include:
   - Tiering
   - Reimbursement adjustments
   - Bonus payments
5. P4P systems generate data that might also be made available to consumers via "data transparency."
6. Common hospital programs look at:
   - Hospital-specific clinical measures
   - Patient safety
   - Patient satisfaction
   - The use of IT
7. Common physician programs look at:
   - Groups of physicians rather than individual physician performance
   - Physician-oriented clinical measures

Notes

- Patient satisfaction
- The use of IT
- Physician recognition by NCQA

8. Medicare is experimenting with several demonstrations of P4P in nonmanaged FFS Medicare.

Notes

CHAPTER 9

Managing Basic Medical/Surgical Utilization

CHAPTER STUDY REVIEW

1. One of the principal objectives of utilization management is the reduction of practice variation by establishing parameters for cost-effective use of healthcare resources. The techniques used to manage utilization serve to contain cost while ensuring the provision of appropriate care.
2. MCOs have enjoyed a high rate of return on their investment in utilization management activities in the form of lower healthcare costs.
3. Demand management is a set of activities designed to reduce the overall requirement for healthcare services by members. These activities can include:
   - **Nurse advice lines**. These provide members with access to advice on medical conditions, the need for medical care, health promotion and preventive care, and similar health-related activities.
   - **Self-care and medical consumerism programs**. The provision of information to members to enable them to provide care for themselves or better evaluate when they need to seek care from a professional.
   - **Shared decision-making programs**. These programs involve making patients active participants in choosing their courses of care.
   - **Medical informatics**. This broad term applies to the use of information technology in the management of healthcare delivery.
   - **Preventive services and health-risk appraisals**. Common preventive services include immunizations, mammograms, routine physical examinations and health assessment, and counseling regarding behaviors that members can undertake to lower their risk of ill health. A health-risk appraisal tool elicits information from a member regarding certain activities and behaviors that can influence health status.
4. The two primary means of measuring utilization are physician utilization data and hospital utilization data. With regard to physician

Notes

utilization data, there is no set standard for reporting data on referral utilization. Counting only the initial referral or authorization might result in missing a large portion of actual utilization. With regard to hospital utilization data, a choice must be made as to what will be measured and how that measurement will be defined. Hospital utilization data can vary by geography and by practice.

5. Electronic connectivity and the incorporation of evidence-based medicine to pay-for-performance systems is rising.
6. The PCP plays a key role in utilization management at HMOs. In this type of authorization system, a member might visit a PCP without any barriers to access, but to see a specialist the member must obtain authorization from the PCP. In certain circumstances—usually those in which a member has a chronic disease—it is better for a specialist to act as PCP. If the member does not obtain PCP authorization, the plan might not pay for unauthorized services (HMO plans) or might offer a lower level of payment (POS plans). Many managed care plans have done away with PCP authorization systems, however, even in HMOs. PPOs and other types of plans do not rely on PCP authorization systems.
7. The six types of authorization are:
   - Prospective, also called Pre-Certification
   - Concurrent
   - Retrospective
   - Pended for review
   - Denial
   - Subauthorization
8. Three common methods for managing utilization are:
   - **Prospective review**. The review of cases before they happen.
   - **Concurrent review**. The review of cases while they are active.
   - **Retrospective review**. The review of cases after they are finished.
9. Health plans frequently assign a maximum length of stay.
10. The role of the UM nurse can include one or more of the following:
    - Information gathering
    - Telephone rounding
    - Hospital rounding
    - Review against criteria
    - Discharge planning and follow-up
11. Physicians can take on the following roles:
    - PCP
    - SCP
    - Hospitalist
    - Medical director

Notes

12. The ED must be managed separately.

13. Alternatives to inpatient care include:
- Subacute care
- Step-down units
- Outpatient procedure units
- Hospice
- Home health care

Notes

CHAPTER 10

Fundamentals and Core Competencies in Disease Management

CHAPTER STUDY REVIEW

1. The premise behind disease management (DM) is that chronic conditions, although representing a relatively small number of plan members, represent the majority of costs. This is expected to increase as baby boomers age.
2. Disease management includes the following components:
   - Population identification processes
   - Evidence-based practice guidelines
   - Collaborative practice models to include physicians and support providers
   - Patient self-management education
   - Process and outcomes measurement
   - Routine reporting and a feedback loop
3. Disease management can be performed by a health plan or by a DM company. Build versus buy is a common issue for health plans.
4. The following are elements essential to most DM programs:
   - Condition prioritization
   - Participant identification
   - Recruitment and engagement
   - Interaction and management
   - Outbound calls to participants
   - Mailings to participants
   - Inbound calls from participants
   - Outbound calls to physicians
   - Mailings to physicians
   - Inbound calls from physicians
   - Home telemonitoring
   - Medication adherence technology

Notes

5. It is difficult to accurately measure the effectiveness of such programs, and ROI has been the single-most controversial element of DM.
6. Challenges of the current DM model include:
   - Privacy requirements
   - Meaningful engagement between affected parties
   - Physician integration
7. Incentives for participants and even physicians are an element of many DM programs.
8. DM programs require rigorous reevaluation on a regular basis so as to eliminate activities that are no longer productive while adding new activities as they evolve.

Notes

Chapter 11

Case Management

CHAPTER STUDY REVIEW

1. Case management is the process of evaluating a patient in a fully integrated way and addressing the full spectrum of services required to meet the patient's needs during the acute phase of illness as well as at discharge.

   Case managers work in a variety of settings in both the provider and health-plan side. On the provider side, case managers might work in hospitals, clinics, home health agencies, and provider-sponsored disease management programs. On the health-plan side, case managers perform functions similar to provider-based case managers, while managing the fiduciary obligations of the health plan. Regardless of the setting, the case manager's skill set and preparation are critical to his or her success.
2. Case managers must possess three major categories of characteristics in order to be successful in their profession:
   - Strong clinical expertise and critical-thinking skills
   - Strong interpersonal communication skills
   - A collaborative relationship with physicians and colleagues, born out of mutual trust and respect
3. Successful case managers will be able to deal with patients/families/physicians and be able to actively listen, negotiate, debate, and handle disagreements, controversies, and money issues. They need to be able to keep their own reactions in check when faced with difficult situations.
4. Many providers and health plans are utilizing case managers to assist with the task of managing complex cases, usually those involving high-risk and high-cost patients.
5. Discharge planning needs to begin when a patient enters an acute care facility. For most hospitals, one of the primary points of entry is the emergency department (ED), which is becoming the new front door.
6. DRG-based payment reimbursement is becoming the norm. Health-care providers must manage these dollars very judiciously in order to just break even.

Notes

7. The availability of alternative levels of care is an essential component of a patient's discharge plan. The interdisciplinary team needs to be familiar with the criteria that drive the selection of postacute services that might be required at the time of discharge in order to ensure a safe transition home or to any other postacute discharge setting.
8. Pathways and Protocols are tools that assist the interdisciplinary team in helping the patient to achieve optimal recovery in the least amount of time while making effective use of clinical resources. They also are an excellent way of achieving measurable goals for patient care outcomes.
9. Hospitalists and intensivists are excellent resources. They have a positive impact on resource utilization and on a patient's transition to the appropriate level of care. Studies have shown that the use of these highly trained physicians has contributed to the decrease in the overall patient length of stay (LOS) while providing quality care and continuity of care for the hospitalized patient.
10. HIPAA stands for the Health Insurance Portability and Accountability Act. Patients' Protected Healthcare Information, or PHI, can only be released without authorization for reasons related to treatment, payment, and healthcare operations.

Notes

CHAPTER 12

Prescription Drug Benefits in Managed Health Care

CHAPTER STUDY REVIEW

1. Prescription drug benefits are offered in more than 92% of managed care plans.
2. In 2006, Medicare Part D began offering prescription drug benefits.
3. The goal of managing the prescription drug benefit is to address the supply cost and the utilization demand.
4. Pharmacy benefit management has reduced drug benefit costs by 25% to 45%.
5. Novel challenges include:
    - Medicare Part D
    - Injectable biologic medications—specialty pharmacy
    - CDHPs
6. Possible solutions to these challenges include:
    - Increasing the use of generic drugs
    - Raising prescription copayments and coinsurance
    - Limiting access to certain drugs
    - Using closed formularies
7. Pharmacy information services include:
    - Pharmacy claims adjudication
    - Pharmacy and medical claims integration and clinical program support
    - Electronic prescribing
8. Drug benefits typically exclude or reduce coverage for the following:
    - Experimental drugs
    - FDA-approved drugs used for unapproved indications
    - Drugs used for cosmetic reasons
    - Brand-name drugs for which there is an acceptable generic substitute
    - Drugs available over the counter

Notes

9. Drug reimbursement to a pharmacy is made up of:
   - Drug reimbursement plus or minus a percentage of the Average Wholesale Price (AWP)
   - A dispensing fee
   - Member copayment or coinsurance
10. Specialty pharmacy management is unique and is usually separate from the management of othcr drugs.
11. The Pharmacy and Therapeutics Committee addresses drug formulary development and management.
12. Copayments may be tiered, with greater benefits for generic drugs than brand-name drugs.
13. Some manufacturers have rebate programs in which health plans or employers receive a rebate based on the volume at which a certain drug is prescribed.
14. Measurement of the effectiveness of a pharmacy management program includes the following:
   - Total cost of the program
   - Prescription utilization for selected highly utilized therapeutic categories
   - Generic dispensing rate
   - Drug formulary conformance rate
   - Patient satisfaction
   - Number of prior authorization requests and times for approval
   - HEDIS reports
   - Trend in overall performance

Notes

CHAPTER 13

Managed Behavioral Healthcare Organizations

CHAPTER STUDY REVIEW

1. Nonpsychiatrists write 75% to 80% of prescriptions for behavioral health medications.
2. Between 1971 and 2001, national expenditures on behavioral health fell from 11.1% to 5.9%.
3. Depressive and anxiety disorders are very common, but frequently undiagnosed.
4. Behavioral health management begins with establishing a network of contracted providers, though usually with somewhat differing access standards.
5. Reimbursement for behavioral health services largely parallels methods used for other health services.
6. Types of behavioral health services include:
   - Inpatient services
   - Residential treatment
   - Partial hospitalization
   - Intensive outpatient treatment
   - Regular outpatient treatment
   - Employee assistance programs
7. Public-sector networks, such as Medicaid, also focus on:
   - Supervised living
   - Programs for assertive community treatment
   - Peer support
   - Continuous treatment teams
   - Community case management
8. Standardized assessment tools commonly are used in day-to-day clinical operations.
9. Management of utilization has evolved over the years, with the goal of reducing the administrative burden on providers.

Notes

10. Only 5% of patients account for 53% of claims spent.
11. Hundreds of measures of quality and effectiveness have been developed, including HEDIS measures.
12. Quality-based incentives are beginning to be introduced to providers.

Notes

CHAPTER 14

Disease Prevention and Health Plans

CHAPTER STUDY REVIEW

1. Prevention can be defined as "action taken to decrease the chance of getting a disease or condition." The goals of disease prevention are to improve health, to save lives, and to save money.
2. Disease-prevention strategies have produced major improvements in longevity and quality of life (e.g., safe drinking water, polio vaccination, and breast cancer screening).
3. Three levels of disease prevention are commonly recognized in health care:
   - Primary prevention is the prevention of disease before it starts.
   - Secondary prevention is the early detection of disease, before the disease becomes symptomatic.
   - Tertiary prevention is the prevention of complications of a chronic disease after the disease is diagnosed.
4. Chronic diseases have replaced infectious diseases as the leading causes of death and illness—and healthcare costs. Heart disease and cancer top the list: together they account for an estimated 1.2 million deaths each year.
5. Most chronic diseases are partially or even entirely preventable by modifying behavioral factors. Tobacco use and the combination of unhealthy diet and physical inactivity are the top two actual (root) causes of death in the United States. Together these factors account for one-third of all deaths (18.1% from tobacco use and 15.2% from diet and inactivity).
6. A strong health plan prevention program includes four components:
   - Appropriate member benefits, such as immunizations and screenings
   - Appropriate member services, such as health-risk assessments and behavior change programs
   - Prevention-oriented provider contracts that lead to system improvements

Notes

- Advocacy for effective public policies, such as increases in the taxes on tobacco products

7. Public policies are the single most effective approach to primary prevention, because they influence an entire population on a daily basis. Childhood immunizations ("no shots, no school") and clean indoor air laws ("smoking bans" that include bars and restaurants as well as other workplaces) are two examples of highly effective public policies that prevent future disease and improve health.
8. Health plans that lead or collaborate on lobbying efforts for effective prevention strategies demonstrate visible public leadership and active concern for their members' health. Public policy advocacy is a relatively new role for health plans, but one that might gain traction as health plan executives, purchasers, and other community leaders realize the cost-effectiveness of this approach.

Notes

CHAPTER 15

Quality Management in Managed Care

CHAPTER STUDY REVIEW

1. The Institute of Medicine's Committee on the Quality of Health Care in America proposed six aims for healthcare system improvements in its report Crossing the Quality Chasm (2001):
   - **Safe**. Avoid injuring patients through the care that is intended to help them (e.g., medication errors and surgery on the wrong organ/part).
   - **Effective**. Provision of services to all who could benefit based on scientific knowledge and refraining from providing services to those not likely to benefit (e.g., treatment of a common cold with antibiotics).
   - **Patient centered**. Providing care that is respectful of and responsive to patient preferences, needs, and values.
   - **Timely**. Reducing waits and sometimes harmful delays for both those who receive and provide care.
   - **Efficient**. Avoiding waste, including waste of equipment, supplies, ideas, and energy.
   - **Equitable**. Providing care that does not vary in quality because of personal characteristics such as gender, ethnicity, geographic location, and socioeconomic status.
2. The five traditional criteria for healthcare quality assessment are as follows:
   - Structural measures of healthcare performance are focused on the context in which care and services are provided.
   - Process-of-care measures evaluate the way in which care is provided.
   - Most outcome measurements focus on measurements of infection rates, morbidity, and mortality.
   - Peer review centers on a comparison of an individual provider's practice either with practice by the provider's peers or with an acceptable standard of care.

Notes

- Appropriate evaluation includes a review of the extent to which the MCO provides timely, necessary care at the right level of service.

3. External customers of MCOs include members or benefactors and purchasers. The departments and services in the MCOs are the internal customers.
4. Customers want to know whether an MCO meets their expectations. In addition, purchasers and members value access and appropriateness. Also of import to purchasers are value assessments of disease-screening activities, service quality, and encounter outcomes. In addition, to maintain health and functional capacity, MCOs must support prevention of illness and management of health status. The three key steps in identifying processes and outcomes that meet customer needs are:
   - Treating disease
   - Managing health
   - Ensuring service quality
5. A key step in the performance improvement process is to assess plan performance compared with professional or "best-of-class" standards. This includes appropriateness evaluation, peer review, benchmarking, and outcomes assessment.
6. Legislators and politicians increasingly are acting as advocates for consumers in demanding freedom of choice and access to treatment. As consumerism in managed health care rises, it will be increasingly necessary for MCOs to identify and satisfy consumer needs and demands.

Notes

CHAPTER 16

Data Analysis and Provider Profiling in Health Plans

CHAPTER STUDY REVIEW

1. Data analysis is an increasingly important health plan function. Employers are facing annual cost increases two to three times the consumer price index and are seeking ways to mitigate this trend. Third-party consultants that specialize in data analysis and that aggregate data across health plans also are pressuring health plans to provide actionable information to employers and to use insights from data analysis to improve medical management practices.
2. Data warehousing is a method for standardizing and storing data used for operational purposes (to pay providers of medical services). It is a necessary first step to any analysis effort using claims data.
3. By necessity, the focus of health plan analytics is administrative claims data. The strengths of using administrative claims data for analysis are:
   - Universal language in health plan business
   - Ability to compare data from multiple entities (providers, health plans, government agencies, etc.)
   - Readily available and inexpensive because they have already been collected for payment purposes

   The weaknesses of using administrative claims data for analysis are:
   - Do not contain clinical data found in medical charts; therefore measures mostly process rather than care outcomes
   - Issues with validity and reliability
   - Requires standardizing and storing in a data warehouse, which takes resources, and increases the potential for error as business rules are applied
4. Risk adjustment is an important first step in comparing populations on outcomes related to quality of care. The goal of risk adjustment is to separate treatment effects from inherent member characteristics.
5. There are several requirements for useful data:
   - Data must be clean.

Notes

- Data must be valid.
- Data must be from an appropriate sample size.
- Data must encompass an adequate time period.
- Data from multiple sources should be linked appropriately.
- Data must be consistent and mean the same thing from provider to provider.

6. HIPAA created a stringent minimum set of privacy and security standards for protecting the confidentiality of patient information. Implementation regulations for electronic business transactions include detailed technical specifications based on ANSI X 12N transaction standards.
7. Employers are interested in how their paid-claims trend compares to those of other employers in the same industry. They want to know the main causes for cost increases and what they can do to address them.
8. When using provider profiles to affect quality improvement, the two types of variables that can be profiled are those that relate to costs and those that have a closer relationship to the traditional understanding of quality. Customers and users of provider profiles include managed care organizations, enrollees, employers, and providers.
9. Provider profiles are compared to two sets of norms: internal and comparative. Internal norms are used only if the plan has enough enrollees or patients. Comparative norms use external data.
10. Health plans face increasing pressure for public reporting of both cost and quality data, but the effect of this reporting on consumer and provider behavior is still largely unknown.

Notes

CHAPTER 17

Information Technology in the Health Plan Organization

CHAPTER STUDY REVIEW

1. Although the underlying business of health insurance and health plans is the management of risk, which is actuarially driven, it is IT that provides the ability to execute.
2. IT must not only support ongoing business functions, it must also respond to an evolving market.
3. Critical internal IT capabilities include support for the following:
   - Product design
   - Eligibility
   - Claims processing
   - Medical management and predictive modeling
   - Provider credentialing and network maintenance
   - Member services
   - E-business
4. Delivery attributes of IT include the following:
   - Visibility
   - Security and privacy
   - Usability
   - Flexibility
5. Current market trends that must be supported by IT include the following:
   - Consumerism
   - Pay-for-performance
   - Banking functions
   - Personal health records
6. The following must be addressed when building an IT organization:
   - IT as a business
   - Traditional skills
   - Nontraditional skills

Notes

CHAPTER 18

The Modern Claims Capability

CHAPTER STUDY REVIEW

1. The four primary claims core competencies are transactional processing, quality control, service delivery, and information management. Within each of these core competencies are three integrated components: proven business and communication processes, trained and motivated people, and supporting tools and technology. Weakness in any one component will threaten the entire infrastructure.
2. Auto-adjudication is the process of automatically determining eligibility and correctly applying benefits and payment terms for each claim using predetermined rules without any human intervention.
3. Quality control focuses on functions and processes from initial intake through preparation/staging and concludes with customer service, appeals, and ultimately renewal of the employer group or government contract.
4. Just as business processes and technology are important to transaction processing, so are trained and motivated people who perform the tasks required to process claims, including:
   - Clerical personnel who initially prep paper claims
   - Technically proficient personnel who support EDI transmissions
   - Claims processors who adjudicate claims
   - Supervisors and managers who interpret policies and run daily operations
   - Directors and vice presidents who strategically manage investments in the claims capability
5. Service delivery to members and providers can be handled by claims call centers that respond directly to member and provider claims concerns. Or, the MCO might have a separate call center operation that responds to all member and/or provider inquiries.
6. Information management is the collection and management of data fundamental to the MCO and its customers.

Notes

7. Shared across the four claims capability core competencies are the following common, enterprise-wide objectives:
   - Enabling the MCO to meet contractual obligations to employer groups, government agencies, members, and providers
   - Ensuring timely benefits administration for enrolled members, including the accurate application of cost-sharing features, benefit limitations, maximums, and exclusions
   - Administering medical management policies and medical necessity decisions
   - Improving the health care of its members through the development and execution of care management plans
   - Providing prompt and accurate customer service to members, brokers, employer groups, and providers
   - Protecting financial liability by validating eligibility, avoiding duplicate and other inappropriate claims, ensuring accurate processing, administering other party liability programs, pursuing cost-containment activities related to known or specific financial leakage, and ensuring timely productivity to avoid processing penalties and interest payments
8. Whether claims are submitted on paper or electronically, inventory receipts must be measured in order to allocate adequate resources and verify financial assumptions about an insured population. Other measures important to track include:
   - Timely filing limits
   - Turnaround time based on the date the MCO received the claim
   - "Claims lag," the time elapsed by comparing the date of service to the date of receipt
   - "Incurred but not reported" (IBNR) claims, measured by comparing outstanding authorization records ordering care and other unreported encounters to actual claims received
9. More sophisticated quality review efforts, better analysis, and more flexible reporting have enabled many MCOs to pursue focused, but effective, cost-containment programs designed to curb financial leakage.
10. Outsourcing is an option exercised by many large commercial MCOs and more recently by smaller organizations and nonprofits that wish to reduce costs and improve service levels.
11. Regardless of the type of claim or how it is submitted, the same core claims capability business steps apply: determination of liability, other party liability, benefits administration, application of provider fee schedules, resubmissions, appeals and adjustments, and fraud and abuse.
12. Ultimately, the claims capability is a service organization. If management and business practices are executed with service to internal and external customers in mind, the claims capability will ensure its own health and vitality as well the financial health of its MCO.

Notes

CHAPTER 19

Member Services

CHAPTER STUDY REVIEW

1. The member services and consumer affairs department serves several key functions:
   - Help members understand how to use the plan
   - Help resolve members' problems and/or questions
   - Monitor and track the nature of member contacts
   - Allow members to express dissatisfaction with their care
   - Help members seek review of claims that have been denied or covered at a lower than expected level of benefits
   - Manage members' problems with payments
   - Help address routine business issues
2. The physical location for member services will vary based on factors such as:
   - Real estate costs
   - Wage rates
   - Telecommunications and IT infrastructure
   - Availability of an educated workforce
   - Availability of manager candidates
3. Although exact training and staffing requirements vary by plan, all plans should include new-employee training processes; staffing ratios based on the plan's complexity, growth rate, and size; and the degree of automated support.
4. Special considerations in member services include hours of availability and the ability to meet the needs of non–English speakers.
5. Member services can be accessed by the following modes of communication:
   - Interactive voice response
   - Telephone
   - Mail and paper-based forms
   - E-mail
   - Web chat
   - Internet self-service
6. Reasons for contact include:
   - Claims issues

Notes

- Benefits issues, including appeals and denials
- Enrollment issues
- Provider access issues, primarily in HMOs

7. The member services department helps members use the plan and disseminates information to the membership. The department provides information on such plan aspects as hours of availability and the availability of non–English communications. The department also helps with claims issues, including appeals and denials of payment, enrollment and the issuance of identification cards, and the selection of primary care physicians and access to the network.
8. The member services department can take a proactive stance through outreach programs, including contacting members to discuss the way the plan works, mailing information packs to members, and establishing telephone-based information systems.
9. Workforce management includes measures such as:
   - Average speed to answer
   - Service-level percentages
   - Abandonment rates
   - Schedule adherence
   - Average handle time
   - First-call resolution
10. Collection, collation, and analysis of data also fall under the purview of the member services department. Member satisfaction data can be garnered through surveys and direct mail campaigns. Trends analysis can help identify random versus widespread problems. Appropriate data usually are obtained through automated tracking systems.
11. Proactive approaches to member services include the implementation of member education programs, the solicitation of member suggestions and recommendations, and the provision of a wide variety of special services, affiliations, and health promotion activities.
12. Member services might also support data transparency to members regarding healthcare costs, quality, and outcomes.
13. The member services department also handles member complaints and grievances. Complaints are episodes of dissatisfaction by the member with the plan, whereas grievances are formal complaints demanding resolution by the plan.
14. The process for managing formal appeals is regulated under both state and federal laws and regulations.

Notes

CHAPTER 20

The Impact of Consumerism on Managed Health Care

CHAPTER STUDY REVIEW

1. Healthcare consumerism is driven by several factors:
   - Increases in healthcare costs that negatively impact the employer's bottom line
   - Pressure from advocacy groups on large employers, such as Wal-Mart, to provide health coverage for more employees, including part-time employees
   - The overall growth of consumerism in society
   - Employers demanding that employees have a greater stake in the costs of services and treatment
   - Government tax incentives for individuals to pay for their healthcare expenses through health savings and other tax-advantaged accounts
   - Providers beginning to differentiate their services based on cost and efficiency
   - The increased access to healthcare information offered by technology
2. Although today's healthcare consumers are much more educated and empowered than earlier generations, a gap still exists in providing access to information that will be useful in the healthcare decision-making process. The Baby Boomers are expected to increase the movement toward consumerism as they demand access to quality information and services as well as value for their healthcare dollar.
3. Consumerism is not a single feature or tactic, rather it is a mindset created through a series of integrated plan designs, programs, and services that work together to create an educated, engaged consumer.
4. The components of consumerism include education, engagement, plan design, tax-advantaged accounts, consumer financial responsibility, and transparency.

Notes

5. To remain competitive, MCOs will need to engage in several key practices:
   - Dissemination of meaningful and actionable information on cost and quality
   - Development of innovative products and services that will satisfy consumers' preferences for choice, convenience, and access
   - Provision of decision-support tools and services to help individuals plan for and manage their health
   - Streamlining of administrative functions to keep costs in line and prices competitive
   - Provision of guidance to individuals to help them navigate their way through the healthcare system
6. Providers must embrace consumerism by sharing performance-related information with individuals and health care organizations. As in other industries, providers will begin to compete and must play to their strengths and determine their competitive advantages.
7. At the end of the day, consumerism will help make the healthcare market more affordable by increasing competition and requiring providers and managed care organizations to compete on cost, quality, and value.

Notes

CHAPTER 21

Sales and Marketing

CHAPTER STUDY REVIEW

1. After years of unprecedented merger-and-acquisition activity driving growth in the managed care marketplace, health plans are refocusing on organic growth for two main reasons:
   - Inorganic growth is viewed as having a lower return on investment because of high acquisition costs per member and the hidden reality of higher-than-expected postmerger integration costs.
   - A shift toward consumerism that is influenced by the introduction of new consumer-directed products, Medicare reform, and the onset of individual health insurance offerings.
2. Health plan customer segments generally are based on membership size in the commercial space and include individual, small group (typically 2 to 50 member employers), mid-market (51 to approximately 5,000 members), and large case (more than 5,000 members), with some designation within each of these segments to reflect the risk arrangement and the product portfolio purchased. Additionally, many health plans have organizations and products focused on serving the government-sponsored Medicare and Medicaid markets.
3. The *employer-sponsored* channel is a business-to-business-to-consumer model characterized by heavy reliance on intermediary distribution channels, namely brokers and consultants. The *direct markets* channel, which includes Medicare and individual commercial offerings, is characterized by a closer relationship with the consumer.
4. More than 85% of employer-sponsored business involves an intermediary, typically a broker or consultant:
   - Brokers typically focus on relatively smaller employers and are compensated based on commissions paid by the health plan.
   - Consultants focus on larger employers and receive fee-based compensation paid by the employer.
5. The key steps in the employer-sponsored sales process include:
   - Lead generation
   - Prospecting
   - Rating and underwriting

Notes

- Quoting
- First sale (to the employer)
- Case installation
- Second sale (to the employee)
- Enrollment

6. Common sales channels for the Medicare and individual markets include:
   - Direct mail to the consumer
   - Field sales executed by internal sales resources or brokers
   - Telesales
   - Web sales
   - Affinity programs with businesses outside of the healthcare space
7. Health plans face several challenges in pursuing sales in the employer-sponsored markets, including:
   - Lack of valuable and usable insight around employers, brokers, and members
   - Historic underinvestment in sales and account management resources
   - Commoditization of products, networks, and services, reducing differentiation in the marketplace
   - Array of unpredictable influences on health plan purchasing decisions, including input from brokers, consultants, other employers, providers, employees, and governments
   - High degree of seasonality in employer healthcare purchasing, causing resource fluctuations
8. Direct-market challenges include consumer insight gaps, immature market-facing tools (e.g., Web-based channels), and regulatory protections of consumer data and engagement.
9. Despite formidable challenges, some health plans are demonstrating high-performance selling in pursuing organic growth:
   - Transformation from a reactive, transactional, service-focused model to a proactive, consultative, strategic model focused on growth
   - Incorporating performance metrics borrowed from retail paradigms, such as "share of wallet" and "cost to sell"
   - Reducing the time frame from the time of sale to fulfillment by closing process gaps and eliminating redundancies in the sales process
   - Employing distribution channel loyalty programs to drive higher productivity from distribution partners
   - Creating centralized RFP units to drive efficiencies to the common practice of employer RFP response

Notes

- Investing in customer insight and analytics to drive toward a deeper understanding of health plan membership

10. High performance in direct market sales is characterized by online sales, marketing automation, and advanced telesales technology.
11. The advent of new products, particularly in the consumer-directed and Medicare spaces, has demanded a dramatic increase in marketing spending and improvement in health plan marketing capabilities.
12. Key health plan marketing functions include:
    - Brand management
    - External communications
    - Advertising
    - Market research
    - Lead generation
    - Sales campaign support
13. High-performing health plan marketing organizations are able to:
    - Measure and grow the value of the health plan's brand
    - Measure and optimize marketing spending across a portfolio
    - Deliver advanced consumer segmentation
    - Plan and execute targeted consumer campaigns

Notes

CHAPTER 22

The Employer's View of Managed Health Care

CHAPTER STUDY REVIEW

1. Managed care trends affect stakeholders—consumers, providers, employers, health plans, and the government—in a variety of ways. The main trends affecting these groups are restructuring; increased competition within healthcare markets and across other industry sectors, such as the financial sector; the growing prevalence of consumerism; increasing healthcare costs; the renewed focus on defining and measuring quality; and the advent of Medicare Part D.
2. Market trends affect large, medium, and small employers in different ways. Large employers are trying to regain their leverage with a rapidly consolidating group of national health plans. Medium-sized employers are still significantly price sensitive and represent a growth area for the national plans, so competition is fierce. Small employer groups are the most price sensitive and will be affected by continued price increases. Consumer-driven health care is quite popular with this group.
3. The concept of value continues to evolve. It is no longer a simple cost–quality equation. It is more about the alignment of cost and care management interventions for a certain employee population that will produce the most cost-efficient outcomes as measured by evidence-based guidelines. The most tailored alignment of interventions is for large employers, but even small employers are reaping the benefits of reengineered care management programs and targeted interventions from their health plans.
4. The value definition used to be focused on the employer, but now it is increasingly focused on the employee. In fact, the two are inextricably linked. This linkage started with the understanding of the impact of employee-reward systems, including healthcare benefits on business results. Value now has another component—employee engagement. Although the science of employee engagement is young, the early results are very telling. The more engaged the employee, the more

Notes

likely the employee is to comply with the healthcare program. This lowers the employer's healthcare costs, increasing the likelihood that the employer will succeed in its business strategy.

5. Seven trends are likely to impact the future of managed care as we know it:
   - Consumerism and technology will remain dominant themes.
   - Government and Medicare Part D will be at full power.
   - Prevention is back and is a valued piece of the care continuum for employers of all sizes.
   - Health and wealth will converge as individuals assume more responsibility and accountability for their own health care, assisted by multiple forms of tax-advantaged healthcare spending accounts.
   - Collaboration and cooperation between medical providers, groups of employers, and researchers will be the only way to advance quality initiatives and adherence to evidence-based guidelines.
   - Healthcare reform around access and coverage of care will be state based, not a national universal plan.
   - Employers will continue to evaluate their role in providing active healthcare benefits for their employees. Retiree health care will almost always be the responsibility of the individual going forward.

Notes

CHAPTER 23

Accreditation and Performance Measurement Programs for Managed Care Organizations

CHAPTER STUDY REVIEW

1. Since 1991, accreditation and performance measurement have become enduring features in the managed care landscape. Driven by mandates from employers, state and federal government, consumers, and a desire by health plans to objectively demonstrate their quality, a majority of the nation's health maintenance organizations (HMOs) and point-of-service (POS) health plans now participate in some form of accreditation. During this same period, the oversight process has evolved from its initial focus on HMOs to include accreditation, certification, and performance measurement programs that cover the full spectrum of affiliated healthcare organizations.
2. The National Committee for Quality Assurance (NCQA) is an independent group that accredits and certifies a wide range of healthcare organizations, including managed care plans, managed behavioral healthcare organizations, physician organizations, and credentials verification organizations. Health plan review teams consist of one to two administrative and three or four physician reviewers. Plans are reviewed in the areas of:
   - Quality improvement
   - Processes for reviewing and authorizing medical care
   - Delegation
   - Quality of provider network
   - Member rights and responsibilities
   - HEDIS clinical performance measures
   - CAHPS surveys of member experience

Notes

3. HEDIS is a set of standardized measures developed and maintained by NCQA that examine plan performance across a variety of areas. HEDIS specifies what to measure and how to measure it. Areas covered by HEDIS include:
   - Effectiveness of care
   - Access to or availability of care
   - Satisfaction with the experience
   - Health plan stability
   - Use of services
   - Health plan descriptive information

   More than 90% of HMOs and POS plans report on HEDIS; those that report have seen steady, and sometimes dramatic, performance improvements.
4. NCQA reports plan performance to the public using five categories: access and service, qualified providers, staying healthy, getting better, and living with illness. They are used in online report cards and "America's Best Health Plans," a collaboration with U.S. News & World Report to rank commercial, Medicare, and Medicaid managed care plans.
5. Beyond HMOs and POS plans, NCQA offers several additional certification and accreditation programs, including those for disease management, managed behavioral healthcare organizations, PPOs, CVOs, new health plans that would not otherwise qualify for NCQA accreditation participation, and physician organization certification.
6. The Utilization Review Accreditation Commission (URAC) was founded in response to the concerns and frustration with the diversity of utilization review (UR) procedures and the growing impact of UR on physicians and hospitals. URAC's UM standards can be applied to stand-alone UM organizations or to UM functions that are integrated into health benefits programs. URAC now uses only its initials as its name.
7. URAC's core accreditation standards reflect the quality of the basic healthcare functions of an organization. Standards fall into the following categories:
   - Organizational structure
   - Personnel management
   - Operations and processes
   - Quality improvement
   - Delegation of responsibilities
   - Consumer protection
8. URAC also offers accreditation programs in the areas of health utilization management, health networks, quality management, disease management, health provider credentialing, and health Web sites.
9. The Accreditation Association for Ambulatory Health Care (AAAHC) accredits more than 2,700 healthcare organizations, including endoscopy centers, ambulatory surgery centers, student health centers,

Notes

and medical and dental health centers. Core AAAHC accreditation standards apply to all organizations seeking accreditation; adjunct standards apply to organizations based on the services they provide. Core standards include:

- Rights of patients
- Governance
- Administration
- Quality of care provided
- Quality management and improvement
- Clinical records and health information
- Facilities and environment

10. Organizations surveyed by the AAAHC are awarded one of five accreditation statuses by the AAAHC Accreditation Committee after review: 3-year accreditation, 1-year accreditation, 6-month accreditation, deferred decision, or denial/revocation of accreditation.

Notes

CHAPTER 24

Operational Finance and Budgeting

CHAPTER STUDY REVIEW

1. An MCO's product-pricing strategies form the basis of its overall financial management. After the establishment of pricing strategies, an MCO develops a detailed operating budget.
2. Although MCOs are regulated primarily at the state level, federal regulations might be imposed when an MCO offers a federally regulated product such as Medicare risk contracts. Publicly held MCOs are subject to SEC rules and regulations. Two state-based organizations that have an interest in MCO function are the Department of Insurance and the Department of Health.
3. Financial managers must address the many and varied interests of a variety of people, including senior managers, insurance regulators, the SEC, tax authorities, and investors.
4. Financial statements have five key components:
   - **Operating statement**: A high-level profit and loss statement.
   - **Premium revenue**: The primary revenue source for most MCOs. Premiums are generally received in advance for coverage of a month-long period.
   - **Other revenue sources**: These can include fee revenue from such sources as coordination of benefits recoverable, reinsurance recoverable, and interest income.
   - **Medical expenses**: This covers physician, hospital, and ancillary services and expenses incurred on a capitated basis, fee schedule, or per diem arrangement.
   - **Administrative expenses**: These include salaries and sales, marketing, and other operating expenses.
5. A balance sheet includes seven basic elements:
   - **Cash and investments**: This represents a significant portion of the MCO's balance sheet.
   - **Premium receivable**: Premiums usually are collected monthly.
   - **Other assets**: A typical large asset may be fixed assets.

Notes

- **Unearned premiums**: Premiums received by the MCO at the close of the financial reporting period that have not been earned, usually because they have been paid in advance.
- **Claims payable and IBNR**: The basis for recording claim reserves depends on information provided by other operating areas of the MCO.
- **Risk-pool liabilities**: Reimbursement strategies may involve risk pools. In these instances, MCOs must maintain accurate records of payments withheld from physicians and hospitals.
- **Equity**: MCOs must track both SAP and GAAP basis equity.

6. MCOs are subject to certain regulatory reporting considerations. Depending on the type of plan, an MCO will have to submit quarterly financial statements, annual statements, Schedules D and L, certification on claims reserves, and audited financial statements.

7. Financial forecasts predict activity and results beyond the current period and are important financial management tools. They often are developed several months in advance of the reporting period. In generating forecasts, the financial manager seeks a balance between simplicity of a summary level and complexity of the actual details required.

8. In July 2002, the president signed Sarbanes-Oxley into law. The act came in response to a string of corporate scandals, including the collapse of a number of businesses that negatively affected the confidence of investors in the capital markets of the United States. The act's focus is on investor-owned companies (not specifically health insurance). It contains 11 titles (sections), ranging from board responsibilities to "whistleblower" protections to penalties. Most important, it created the Public Company Accounting Oversight Board (PCAOB), a quasi-government agency that oversees the audits of public companies, intending to protect investors' interests and other users of an issuer's financial statements.

With regard to financial management, Section 404 of the act has two parts: Section 404(a) describes management's responsibility for establishing and maintaining an adequate internal control structure and procedures of financial reporting. It also outlines management's responsibility for assessing the effectiveness of internal control over financial reporting. Section 404(b) describes the independent auditor's responsibility for attesting to and reporting on management's internal control assessment.

Notes

CHAPTER 25

Underwriting and Rating Functions

CHAPTER STUDY REVIEW

1. Ideally, underwriting and rating create a balance among factors such as adequacy, competitiveness, and equity of rates.
   - Adequate rates are high enough to generate sufficient revenue to cover all claims and other plan expenses and yield an acceptable return on equity.
   - Competitive rates are low enough to sell enough policies and enroll enough members to meet health plan volume and growth targets.
   - Equitable rates will approximate any given group's costs without an unreasonable amount of cross-subsidization among groups.
2. Effective underwriting focuses on four areas:
   - Health status
   - Ability to pay premium
   - Other coverage (if applicable)
   - Historical persistency
3. Rating uses information gathered through underwriting to calculate the premium for a specific individual or group. The premium calculation is generally done using a rate formula, historical experience, predictive underwriting tools, or some combination of these.
4. The rate formula should recognize all health plan costs, be easy to apply in the majority of situations, and result in an appropriate premium rate. Rates are typically expressed on a per member per month (PMPM) basis that is adjusted to contract rates in group situations.
5. The rate formula provides the mechanism to adjust the base rate to a group-specific premium. The formula adjusts the base rate based on demographics, area, group size, and other characteristics to arrive at a manual rate specific to a group or individual.
6. Incurred claims, which are calculated through the conversion of paid claims data, are matched with health plan exposure (measured in

Notes

member months) to develop a base period PMPM cost when experience is available.

7. Rate formula adjustments should consider relevant, measurable factors that predict medical cost differences among individuals/groups, but the formula should still be easy to measure and apply.
8. Experience is the best data source for health plans. Plans lacking credible experience refer to published sources or actuarial consulting firms for initial medical cost targets.
9. Rate formulas are updated using data from management reports such as financial gain/loss summaries, incurred claims costs, group-specific information, a development of incurred but unreported claims, and membership information.

Notes

CHAPTER 26

Health Plans and Medicare

CHAPTER STUDY REVIEW

1. Medicare has been a federal entitlement program since 1965. It was significantly modified in 2003 with the Medicare Prescription Drug Improvement and Modernization Act of 2003, which added a new voluntary drug benefit called Part D. It also changed the old Medicare+Choice program to the new Medicare Advantage (MA) program.
2. The drug benefit is provided by private plans, either prescription drug plans (PDPs) or Medicare Advantage Prescription Drug (MA-PD) plans.
3. The benefit design of Part D provides greater coverage for the first $2,500 (after a deductible), no coverage for the next $2,600, then greater coverage for expenses higher than that. These numbers were for 2007, and change from year to year.
4. PDPs and MA-PDs are allowed to offer greater coverage, but cannot offer less coverage.
5. The basic beneficiary premium is the product of a bidding mechanism by plans. A subsidy is provided for low-income beneficiaries.
6. There is a risk corridor for sharing risk and reward between CMS and plans, although this will decrease up until 2011. What will occur after that has not been determined.
7. New MA plans are to be regional PPOs. Existing HMOs previously under Medicare+Choice became MA-Local plans.
8. There are many types of MA plans:
   - PPOs
   - Private fee for service (PFFS)
   - Special needs plans
   - Medical Savings Account plans
   - Employer group plans
9. Payments to plans are established by law and comparison of these payment rates to plan bids is referred to as a competitive bidding system.

Notes

10. Payments to plans are risk adjusted to accommodate adverse selection.
11. MA plans have a number of restrictions and requirements:
    - Quality standards must be maintained.
    - Quality reports, such as HEDIS and CAHPS, must be provided.
    - Incentives to physicians are limited.
12. Consumer protections with regard to MA plans include:
    - Access standards
    - Member appeals and grievances rights
    - Provider protections and prompt-payment requirements
13. Enrollment of beneficiaries takes place during defined periods and events.
14. Enrollment locks a beneficiary into the plan after the first 3 months of enrollment until the next enrollment period.
15. MA plans face a variety of marketing restrictions, including prohibitions against door-to-door marketing.
16. The application process to CMS for MA plans and PDPs is set by law and regulation, with strict adherence to dates and timing.

Notes

CHAPTER 27

Medicaid Managed Care

CHAPTER STUDY REVIEW

1. Medicaid was developed as the principal healthcare program for low-income people. It was originally patterned after private insurance; however, costs were far above estimates, and the program was challenged by rapid growth and medical care cost inflation.
2. States began experimenting with managed care models in the 1980s to address some of the problems endemic to Medicaid. The problems encountered included declining provider participation, limited access to primary and preventive care, dependence on inappropriate sites of care, and concern regarding the quality of services that beneficiaries were able to receive.
3. Managed care arrangements have enabled states to address a number of concerns with their Medicaid programs, but the results have been uneven, reflecting the great variation in how Medicaid is designed, supported, and managed across the country and how successfully Medicaid agencies have embraced managed care contracting.
4. Managed care in Medicaid differs substantially from commercial and Medicare managed care, and this has contributed to growing specialization among plans in the Medicaid market. An increasing percentage of Medicaid participants are enrolled in multistate investor-owned plans that focus solely on Medicaid or in Medicaid-specialized subsidiaries of national multiproduct managed care companies.
5. Several distinctive features of the Medicaid market present operational challenges to those organizations that focus on this product line. These include burdensome administrative demands, populations with few financial resources and high levels of social and/or medical needs, difficulties in assembling provider networks, and uncertain policy and payment environment that varies across states and over time.
6. The climate for continued expansion of Medicaid has been supportive in recent years, and plans participating in the market have done well financially. But plans that have selected Medicaid as a target opportunity are facing rising demands and expectations from state Medicaid purchasers. These demands are in the areas of demonstrating

Notes

systematic quality improvement, providing greater transparency in performance, and extending their services to high-cost beneficiaries, including those that have Medicare as well as Medicaid coverage.

7. Looking into the future, states are likely to ask managed care plans to assist them in addressing some of the persistent problems that have plagued Medicaid since its earliest days. These issues include implementing bona fide pay-for-performance programs for Medicaid providers; designing models of care that integrate physical and behavioral health more completely; addressing the needs of persons requiring long-term care; and experimenting with the means to promote more personal responsibility among Medicaid beneficiaries.

Notes

CHAPTER 28

The Military Managed Care Health System

CHAPTER STUDY REVIEW

1. The MHS managed care plan, TRICARE, offers a range of primary, secondary, and tertiary care benefits to approximately 9.2 million eligible beneficiaries at an annual cost of more than $38.4 billion.
2. A unique aspect of military managed care is the MHS's readiness mission. Readiness is defined as the ability of forces, units, technical systems, and equipment to deliver the output for which they were designed. Readiness also is associated with maintaining the health status of active duty personnel well above the health standing associated with civilian personnel.
3. Military health care traces its origins to the Army Medical Department, which was established by the Continental Congress on July 27, 1775. The Continental Congress also established the fledgling nation's first "Director General and Chief Physician." A 1779 Act passed by the congress that addressed military health care had one unique feature: a directive to collect prospective payments for healthcare services. The act directed the Secretary of the Navy to deduct 20 cents a month from sailors and marines' pay to offset their care in civilian treatment facilities. This might represent the first instance in American managed care history that prepayment for prospective health services was required.
4. In 1834, the Adjutant General ruled that military surgeons had permission to treat civilians when it did not interfere with their required military duties. This policy established the benefit—and later entitlement—to free health care for authorized dependents of service members. More important, this might be the first instance in American health care that nonmonetary benefits (i.e., health care) were granted by an organization to family members of the employed person.
5. In 1956, in an effort to keep up with a growing civilian trend to offer healthcare benefits and entitlements to retired persons, Congress

Notes

enacted the Dependents' Medical Care Act. It provided that, "Medical and dental care in any medical facility of the uniformed services may, under regulations prescribed jointly by the Secretaries of Defense and Health, Education and Welfare, be furnished upon request and subject to the availability of space, facilities, and capabilities of the medical staff, to retired members of uniformed services." The act additionally applied to dependents of uniformed retirees. The significance of the act was that it legitimized standing policies already in widespread application throughout the military health system.

6. In 1994, Congress enacted the National Defense Authorization Act (NDAA). The NDAA directed the DOD to prescribe and implement a health benefit option for beneficiaries eligible for health care under Chapter 55 of Title 10, United States Code (USC). The NDAA also directed the military health system to implement health programs modeled on managed care plans in the private sector. In response to this mandate, the military health system developed the military managed care plan called TRICARE. TRICARE's name was coined to represent the three primary military services involved in providing health care to DOD beneficiaries (Army, Navy and Air Force). The name also represents the three managed care options developed to administer care.
7. TRICARE Prime is the HMO-like plan; beneficiaries enroll in this benefit option where it is offered. TRICARE Standard is the traditional indemnity benefit (also known as fee for service, or FFS), formerly known as CHAMPUS. TRICARE Extra is based on a civilian PPO model in which beneficiaries eligible for TRICARE Standard may decide to use preferred civilian network providers on a case-by-case basis.
8. Since TRICARE's inception, the military managed care system has struggled to balance the elements of Coppola's Managed Care Quaternion (MCQ) and Kissick's Iron Triangle. The Quaternion has been used for several years to help explain the complex interactions among employers, patients, providers, and payers in regard to partisan and competing views about health care. Moreover, these healthcare actors also have dissimilar views regarding Kissick's Iron Triangle. Kissick coined the term Iron Triangle in the 1990s to demonstrate the difficulty in selecting healthcare priorities with regard to healthcare costs, healthcare quality, and access to health care. When juxtaposed together, the two models create a "Parity of Healthcare." Coppola developed the Parity of Healthcare concept and model to assist in explaining to military healthcare leaders why consensus on any single aspect of health care is difficult.

Notes

CHAPTER 29

Managed Care in a Global Context

CHAPTER STUDY REVIEW

1. Private health insurance plays an important role in a wide variety of health systems around the globe, and as these systems struggle with the challenge of balancing coverage, costs, and quality, there is a growing interest in managed care tools and techniques. These managed care functions include the sharing and management of financial risk, development and management of provider networks, management of service utilization, care management, and, increasingly, the management of information flow as well as quality and outcome measurement.
2. Internationally, countries vary tremendously in the financing and organization of their health systems. Some of the dimensions used to make comparisons among different countries include the amount of spending on health care (both as percent GDP and per capita), the source of financing (public vs. private), the type of private financing (out-of-pocket payments vs. prepaid plans), and the percentage of the population covered by government/social insurance plans. When broad measures of countries' health status (such as life expectancy at birth and under-5 child mortality) are examined in the context of health system metrics, we find that there is no "right" way to design a health system. Such comparisons can show important differences; the United States, for example, spends more than every other country without achieving the same level of health status or population coverage as many countries that spend far less.
3. Health systems can be broadly categorized as (1) government sponsored, (2) social insurance model, or (3) private insurance model. Within each health system, the role of private insurance may be the primary means of insurance, or it may substitute, complement, or supplement government-sponsored or social insurance models. Other important considerations are what types of organization(s) are primarily responsible for running the health system and how much of the population is covered.

Notes

4. In low- and middle-income countries, particularly those with a growing middle class, private health insurance can play an important role in providing coverage. This private-sector role may help free up scarce government resources to be focused on the neediest.
5. In higher-income countries, exporting managed care plans wholesale has not met with great success. Though many U.S. managed care companies have tried ventures abroad, few are still in operation. Among the difficulties faced by these companies operating abroad were the complexity of adapting to local conditions, provider resistance, and anti–American or anti-managed-care political sentiment.
6. Many overseas operations of U.S. MCOs provide services to American expatriates working abroad. There may be a considerable market overseas for managed care expertise and tools. U.S. MCOs have developed extensive claims processing and information technology expertise, as well as care management tools and quality metrics, that may be of interest to other health systems.
7. The following factors should be considered when assessing a country's "managed-care readiness":
   - Degree of central/regional government control
   - Current role of private insurance/organizations
   - Choice of health plan
   - Choice of provider
   - Degree of provider integration and organization
   - Degree of financial controls and incentives
   - Population orientation
   - Use of utilization review, evidence-based medicine, and care management

Notes

CHAPTER 30

Legal Issues in Provider Contracting

CHAPTER STUDY REVIEW

1. Despite the wide variations among provider contracts, several issues are common to the contracting process:
    - The managed care plan should identify key objectives that fall into two categories: (1) those that are essential and (2) those that are highly desirable, but not essential.
    - The managed care plan should develop a master schedule that identifies the contracts that must be entered into and renewed.
    - A managed care organization must sometimes develop a letter of intent that defines the basic elements of a contemplated arrangement or transaction between the two parties.
    - The plan should devise a negotiating strategy based on objectives and relative negotiating strength.
2. Despite variations in content, contracts have the same basic structure: a title, a caption, a transition, recitals, definitions, a closing or testimonium, and appended documents or exhibits.
3. Clauses, provisions, and key factors common to most contracts include:
    - **Names**: The names of the parties entering into the agreement are set forth in the initial paragraph.
    - **Recitals**: These are a series of statements that describe who the parties are and what they are trying to accomplish.
    - **Table of contents**: This helps the reader locate pertinent sections within the contract.
    - **Definitions**: This section serves to simplify the reader's understanding of the contract by providing definitions for complicated terms.
    - **Provider obligations**: The obligations cover provider qualifications and credentialing, provider service, nondiscriminatory requirements, compliance with utilization and quality management programs, acceptance of enrollee patients, procedures for

Notes

enrollee complaints, and maintenance and retention of records and confidentiality.

- **Payment**: The payment terms are some of the most important provisions for both providers and managed health care plans. This section covers a number of different payment issues and addresses risk-sharing arrangements, payment and physician–hospital organizations, other-party liability, any other payment-related issues, and hold-harmless and no-balance-billing clauses.
- **Relationship of the parties**: Most contracts state that the managed health care plan and the provider have an independent contractual arrangement.
- **Use of name**: Contracts often limit the ability of either party to use the name of the other by identifying the circumstances in which either party's name may be used.
- **Notification**: The managed health care plan will ensure that it is advised of changes that affect the ability of the provider to meet contractual obligations.
- **Insurance and indemnification**: Insurance provisions may cover both professional liability and general liability coverage. Also common are cross-indemnification provisions.
- **Term, suspension, and termination**: The term section sets forth the term of the contract and of any subsequent contract renewals. Some contracts grant the managed care plan a right of suspension in which the contract continues, but the provider loses specific rights. Termination provisions cover termination without cause and termination with cause.
- **Flow-down clauses and provider subcontracts**: Managed care plans may be obligated to flow down some clauses that are included in the contract between the plan and the payer. If the provider will be subcontracting, the contract should include language to specify whether the plan or the provider will credential subcontracting providers.
- **Declarations**: This section of the contract includes answers to a variety of "what if" questions. Such clauses include force majeure, choice of law provisions, merger clauses, assignment of rights clauses, severability clauses, clauses regarding contract amendments, and clauses regarding the methods through which and to whom notices should be provided.

Notes

CHAPTER 31

ERISA

CHAPTER STUDY REVIEW

1. The Employee Retirement Income Security Act (ERISA) imposes documentation, reporting, and disclosure requirements on employee benefit plans. Each employee benefit plan governed by ERISA is required to describe in a written plan document (or documents) the operative provisions governing benefits under the plan. In addition, each plan participant is entitled to receive a summary plan description, which is a booklet describing the operative provisions of a plan in lay language. The Department of Labor (DOL) has prescribed the types of information that are required to be included in the summary plan description. The plan administrator of an ERISA plan might also be required to file reports with the Internal Revenue Service or the Department of Labor.
2. Plan sponsors have considerable flexibility with respect to the design of their employee benefit plans. ERISA does regulate the content of a limited number of substantive plan provisions, including, but not limited to, provisions relating to compliance with qualified medical child support orders, coverage of adopted children, hospitalization benefits for delivering mothers and newborns, benefits for pediatric vaccines, benefits for breast reconstruction and physical complications related to a mastectomy, preexisting conditions limitations, continuation coverage, eligibility rules, and special enrollment rights.
3. ERISA sets forth the minimum standard of conduct applicable to plan fiduciaries. ERISA's definition of *fiduciary* is functional; that is, a person, regardless of formal title or position, is a fiduciary to the extent that he or she exercises discretionary authority or control over the operation or administration of the plan, exercises any control over plan assets, or renders investment advice for a fee. A fiduciary must discharge his or her obligations with respect to a plan solely in the interests of the plan participants and beneficiaries and for the purpose of providing benefits to plan participants and beneficiaries and defraying reasonable expenses of administering the plan. In addition,

Notes

the fiduciary must act in accordance with the plan documents (except to the extent that the documents are themselves inconsistent with ERISA) and with the care, skill, and diligence that a prudent person familiar with such matters would use. Finally, if the plan is funded, plan investment must be diversified to minimize the risk of large losses.

4. Each employee benefit plan under ERISA is required to establish procedures whereby a plan participant or beneficiary can challenge a denial of his or her claim for benefits. The DOL has promulgated regulations setting forth minimum requirements for employee benefit plan procedures pertaining to claims for benefits by participants and beneficiaries.
5. In addition to suits for benefits brought by a plan participant or beneficiary, ERISA authorizes a plan participant, beneficiary, fiduciary, or the Secretary of the DOL to bring certain civil actions. Among the more important actions are those that involve the right of a plan participant, beneficiary, fiduciary, or the Secretary to bring an action for breach of fiduciary duty. Also, a plan participant, beneficiary, or fiduciary can bring an action to enjoin any act or practice that violates (or to enforce the provisions of) Title I of ERISA or the terms of the plan or to obtain other appropriate equitable relief.
6. ERISA's civil enforcement scheme is exclusive and completely preempts any state law causes of action or remedies that duplicate, supplement, or supplant it.
7. ERISA contains a broad preemption provision, which provides, in relevant part, that any state law that "relates to" any employee benefit plan will be preempted [the preemption clause] unless it is "saved" from preemption because it "regulates insurance" [the savings clause]. ERISA's preemption provision also provides that an employee benefit plan shall not be "deemed" to be an insurance company or to be engaged in the business of insurance for the purposes of any state law purporting to regulate insurance companies [the deemer clause]. The interaction of these three clauses has generated considerable litigation, with the courts generally split as to whether particular causes of actions under state law are preempted under ERISA.
8. Because of the operation of the deemer clause of ERISA's preemption provision, state mandated benefits laws do not apply to self-insured employee benefit plans. However, because of the operation of the savings clause of ERISA's preemption provision, state mandated benefits laws do apply to insurance purchased by employee benefit plans.

Notes

CHAPTER 32

HIPAA

CHAPTER STUDY REVIEW

1. The Health Insurance Portability and Accountability Act (HIPAA) is a federal law that has five major sections:
   - Health care access, portability, and renewability of health insurance
   - Administrative simplification, including the prevention of fraud and abuse
   - Tax-related provisions, including MSAs
   - Application and enforcement of various group health plan requirements
   - Revenue offsets
2. For purposes of the chapter, only Section II is discussed, with a focus on:
   - Privacy
   - Security
   - Electronic transactions
   - Code sets
3. Privacy begins with the definition of what is considered a covered entity under HIPAA. Covered entities include:
   - Health plans
   - All providers of health services
   - Claims clearinghouses
4. Privacy standards require rigorous adherence to policies and procedures to protect protected health information (PHI).
5. Permitted uses of PHI, following certain requirements and limitations, include:
   - For payment, treatment, and healthcare operations
   - For the individual's use
   - For legal, public, and similar activities
   - For business associates covered under certain agreements
   - For plan sponsors
6. The individual has many rights under the privacy provisions.
7. HIPAA requires significant security standards to be met for electronic transactions, including:
   - Security management processes
   - Assigned security responsibility
   - Workforce security

Notes

- Information access management
- Security awareness and training
- Security incident procedures
- Contingency planning
- Evaluation
- Business associate contracts
- Facility access controls
- Workstation use
- Workstation security
- Device and media controls
- Access controls
- Audit controls
- Integrity
- Person or entity identification
- Transmission security

8. Compliance and enforcement of privacy and security requirements rests with the federal government, and potential penalties range from fines to prison sentences.

9. Electronic transactions between covered entities must conform to standards approved by the federal government. Such transactions include:

- Provider claims submission
- Pharmacy claims
- Eligibility
- Claims status
- Provider referral and authorization
- Payment to healthcare providers
- Enrollment and disenrollment of members (not required of employer)
- Claims attachment (near finalization, but rarely used)
- Premium payment to health plan (not required of employer)
- First report of injury (not finalized)

10. Nonstandard electronic transactions may not be used under any circumstances.

11. Code sets used by covered entities for diagnoses and procedures included in electronic transactions must conform to those approved by the federal government, including:

- ICD-9-CM (to be replaced eventually by IDC-10)
- NDC drug codes
- CDP dental codes
- HCPCS and CPT-4

12. HIPAA requires the use of a national provider identifier (NPI) that replaces all other identifiers in use by governmental or private entities, except for the DEA identifier and any tax identifiers. This was implemented in 2007–2008.

Notes

CHAPTER 33

State Regulation of Managed Care

CHAPTER STUDY REVIEW

1. At the state level, HMOs often are regulated by more than one agency—by insurance regulators, who manage financial aspects and, in most states, external review, and by health regulators who focus on quality of care issues, utilization patterns, and a provider's ability to offer adequate care. Risk-bearing PPOs are generally regulated by departments of insurance.
2. State oversight applies to many aspects of MCO operation including:
   - **Licensure**: HMOs obtain licenses by applying for a COA, and applications usually are processed by the insurance department.
   - **Enrollee information**: The HMO Model Act requires certain communications with HMO enrollees. Individual and group contract holders are entitled to receive a copy of their contracts, and regulators require that they are filed with and approved by the regulatory bodies in charge of reviewing contracts. Enrollees also receive an evidence of coverage document, information about how services can be obtained, a list of health plan providers, and notification regarding discontinued participation by the enrollee's PCP. Requirements for similar disclosures to PPO plan enrollees also exist.
   - **Access to medical services**: Under the HMO Model Act, HMOs are required to ensure the availability and accessibility of medical services. The NAIC Network Adequacy Model Act requires MCOs to meet network adequacy standards established by the state.
   - **Provider issues**: The HMO Model Act requires that MCOs applying for state licensure provide regulators with copies of provider contract forms and the names and addresses of all contracted providers. It also requires that contracts include a hold-harmless clause that protects enrollees against provider claims in the event of plan insolvency. In addition, many states require providers to

Notes

include certain provider contract provisions and for claims to be paid within set time frames.

- **Reports and rate filings**: HMOs must file several reports, including annual reports, premium rate schedules, and updates to information contained in the original COA. States may also require HMOs and other MCOs to report on quality and consumer satisfaction.
- **Quality assurance and utilization management**: Several acts dictate HMO procedures regarding quality assurance and utilization management. They require an HMO to file a description of its quality assurance (QA) program; to have in place an internal system that identifies opportunities for improved care, that measures provider performance, that ensures a certain level of provider input, and that collects and analyzes data on over- and underutilization of services; and to have written policies and procedures for credentialing all healthcare professionals.
- **Grievance procedures**: The NAIC Grievance Procedures Model requires that HMOs have written procedures designed to effectively address grievances. In addition, MCOs must comply with Department of Labor claims procedures for dispute resolution for benefit plans subject to ERISA.
- **External appeals**: Most states give enrollees the right to appeal some cases involving the denial of coverage to an external review entity.
- **Solvency standards and insolvency protections**: The HMO Model Act establishes specific capital, reserve, and deposit requirements that all HMOs must meet. This is in order to prevent HMO insolvencies and protect consumers and other parties from the effects of insolvencies.
- **Financial examinations and site visits**: Regulators are able to conduct inquiries that examine HMO finances, marketing activities, and QA programs. The examination process may include site visits.
- **Multisite operations**: MCOs that operate in two or more states must comply with the regulations set forth by each jurisdiction.

3. States have the authority to regulate additional MCO products, including POS offerings, provider-sponsored organizations, specialty HMOs, utilization management organizations, and third-party administrators.
4. Many states have any-willing-provider laws that prohibit MCOs from contracting selectively with all or categories of providers. This has a significant effect on MCOs, because the creation of provider panels is central to basic MCO operations.
5. Many states also have legislation regulating the use of formularies. Such legislation often requires MCOs to disclose their formularies

Notes

and have in place and disclose procedures through which, in certain circumstances, members can obtain nonformulary drugs. Many states have adopted laws that reflect model provisions on drug formularies and procedures for exceptions.

6. Additional state regulations may address physician antitrust exemptions, utilization management, privacy issues, and health plan liability.
7. Many states require MCOs to cover specific services (e.g., clinical trials, congenital defects, in vitro fertilization, TMJ, and ABMT). Some states have begun to look at the implications of mandating health benefits more closely and have created commissions to study the cost-benefit of mandates before they are enacted.